Nylon Road

A Graphic Memoir of
Coming of Age in Iran

Nylon Road

A Graphic Memoir of
Coming of Age in Iran

Parsua Bashi

St. Martin's Griffin

I would like to thank
all of the many people
whose help and support
made this book possible.

♡
To my daughter Abi

I've been living in Zurich since the 23rd of April 2004.

The reason why I came here is another story that I won't explain now.

September 2002 Tehran

I decided to leave Iran and come to Switzerland.

ZURICH AIRPORT

ZURICH CITY

To become ➤ ➤ ➤ "eine weitere Iranerin in Zürich"*

*"Another Iranian in Zurich"

The first days passed very quickly with dinner invitations, wine, champagne, pistachios, and my Swiss friends.

Talking about everything—
art, society, politics,
Iran, Iraq,
Khatami, atomic bombs,
Blocher*, mullahs,
stem cell research,
etc. etc. etc. ...

*Swiss right-wing populist politician

Bush can't bomb my country

...and some sightseeing.

I couldn't manage the daily discipline of practicing calligraphy, so I found another good excuse: The atmosphere in this city does not suit the spiritual needs of a Persian calligrapher...

...at least not in summer.

My English was awful.
It wasn't good enough to read a decent book or magazine.

Nor was it difficult to find excuses to stop practicing German and English. I went back to my Farsi books and hundreds of Farsi websites.

Then I started to feel like a useless asshole, or in the best case like a stupid kid... I was doing nothing.

It was around then that I first saw the little girl.

Since I am not an esoteric type, it was overwhelming to find myself in the same room with myself.

Is she real?

Listen, I want to hear you say something. Anything. Okay? I'm listening

She quietly brought me to the kitchen.

She said that she has always been with me, but that I was the one who had lost contact.

Everybody needs to be in touch with themselves.

Especially with the child in all of us.

In fact, the only reason I'm here is because you called me. I am just a kid and I don't know how all this happened, but if you accept my presence there are more of us waiting to see you. They will be able to explain.

On the one hand I couldn't quite understand what was going on. On the other hand, I could see the whole scene in one instant: I was alone, hopeless, desperate, and apparently unable to deal with the situation. Therefore I called for help. I had to listen to them. They were here to remind me that what I am now is the result of their lives...

and I simply could not deny my past. I had to remember the days and nights I had spent with them—with myself.

I got used to seeing one or more of them from time to time, depending on the situation I happened to be in. One evening, I was listening to the radio to practice my German. I didn't understand everything, but tried anyway.

I tried to explain to her that this is another country with a different history and culture.

Are Europeans so relaxed that they can only talk about things like "ponies" while other people are dealing with shit?!?

Who made the situation like shit? The people themselves or the Europeans?

It's not the Europeans' fault that we had a rotten government. The Swiss deserve their peaceful democracy. They paid the price long ago

Swiss Political History

In a way I could understand her. Besides the war, I thought about all the limitations we had to bear as teenagers compared to the way young people live in Europe today: free and happy.

Oh honey, see how time flies? Just yesterday our daughter was only a baby...

True, very true...

EUROPE

What is your relationship to that sister? Quick, answer!

He's my brother! Believe me Sister. He just came to pick me up from school

You had better not be lying to me

Brother, that sister is my sister...

IRAN

24

28

It was 1984 when I was about 18, five years after the revolution. The fourth year of the Iran-Iraq war. Everybody was trying to flee the country for different reasons. My brother was among the first ones to leave Iran. He was two years older and very close to me. In 1982 our parents found a human smuggler to take him over the Turkish border. He was 17 and had already finished high school. Since the universities were closed,* he would have had to go to the army. That was the last thing our parents wanted.

*The universities were closed between 1980 and 1983 because of the so-called Cultural Revolution

You have to study hard. We will all be together again when this war ends

TURKEY

IRAN

Shortly after that my oldest brother left for the States.

Hey! Come on! Smile! You can come to L.A. as soon as I start earning...

I hate your L.A.!

He was a passionate musician and had no future in Iran.

Music was Haram* at that time, except for the revolutionary marches.

You so-called "musicians"! It's time to find decent jobs for yourselves instead of this satanic occupation!

*forbidden by Islamic law

My best girlfriend left for France the same year we graduated from high school. Then my uncle and his family left for Europe, because they had lost everything in the war. They were living in Ahwaz, which was right at the front. They bought fake visas; I never found out how. My cousins were like sisters to me.

I will write to you every week... I promise!

Hey kids, hurry up! We might miss our flight!

MEHRABAD INTERNATIONAL airport

A close friend from the times when I was still politically active had to leave after he was released from prison. It was a good reason not to stay in Iran. He went illegally to Pakistan where he had to wait for a year for a UN-Refugee permit to go to Sweden. It was hard for me. I had feelings for him, though I had never voiced them.

You'll be my friend, whether we see each other or not... please remember not to say a word about my plan, not to anybody

Of course I won't. Take care of yourself too please, and umm...take this bracelet to remember me by

My cousins and their Italian mother left for Europe since the boys were getting close to the obligatory army-service age.

The boys are too young to live alone in Italy. God knows, leaving their father alone here is the last thing I wanted

He'll join you as soon as he can. The main thing is to protect the boys

Our neighbors, who were like family to us, took the risk of traveling to Turkey where Iranians didn't need a visa, but they had no clear plans. They were expecting a baby in two months. Being Bahai* they had a hard life in post-revolutionary Iran.

We're hoping to get a visa for any European country, then our baby might be born with a European nationality...

But it's dangerous! You are in your seventh month! What if you get stuck in Turkey for months? Then your baby will be a Turk!

* religious minority in Iran

Even my grandmother decided to extend her stay with her children in the States, once she was able to get a visiting visa. She was so scared by the bombing attacks that she got ill.

...and this is for your youngest cousin. She uses this nomadic scarf on Halloween

Yeah, yeah...

Soon, soon...

Will you come back soon?

When?

When my other grandmother left Iran for Europe to live with her son, I realized that although these trips seemed to be temporary, they were seriously tearing families apart, some forever.

IRAN AIRLINES
HOMA
IRANAIR

TERMINAL2 IN

that was her fate: born in Shiraz, died in Göteborg.

30

So I was alone with my parents. It was weird, since we had been a happy family of five, and suddenly we were a family of three with no close relatives or old friends around us.

Do something! It's been more than two months since I've had a letter from the boys...

What can I do? There's war and the post doesn't work like before.

My mother—she was constantly worried about my brothers...

Mum! Muuum! I'm going out! Do you need anything?

...why doesn't he call? What has happened to him? Oh...god...

Puuh

Yes? No! Go then

This is a RED ALARM which means we will be under attack. Go to the shelters!

duuuuuuu duuuuuuu duuuuuu

Hurry up!

Dad! Dad! We should go to the basement. They are bombing!

OK! OK! You go...

...and my father—he drowned himself in work.

The only positive aspect of the soon-to-be-emigrating-people-story was the number of goodbye parties. Although emigration was everyone's concern at the time, I didn't want any part of it.

Who? me?

When are you going to join us and your brothers? You should hurry! We had to work for 18 months to get our documents done!

The Canadian Embassy isn't too busy yet... I'll give you the application forms...

Pah! Not bigger than Cologne, which is the biggest country in the world

We're going to America, the biggest...

But I don't want to leave. I want to study fine arts here in Tehran

Come on! What fine arts?!?

Yeah! Tehran University! With mullahs as teachers? Let alone the terrible national exam. If you pass you'll have to wear a chador*! Good luck!!

* floor-length overgarment worn by Iranian Muslim women

I argued with everybody who was in favor of emigration. I was young; my thoughts and arguments hadn't ripened, but I was strictly against emigration.

They were addressing a truth, though it was bitter to accept. The great wave of emigration had already begun, and lasts through today.

Call me selfish! That's fine! Yes, I'm leaving because I live only once and I'm not going to waste my life on these bloody mullahs!

I'm sorry! I didn't mean you...

One day you'll realize that you made a big mistake to stay in this cursed country!

And yet I hopelessly tried to convince those who were leaving. Partly due to my opinion...

NOooooooo...

...and partly for my own sake. I was abandoned. I was left behind alone!

When none of our family or friends were left, my parents insisted more and more on sending me away. But I remained true to my opinion.

Listen, my daughter. You must join your brothers. I found a way to buy a legal visa to Canada

Dad! Did you forget that I've already passed that really difficult university entrance exam? Now that I've made it, I want to stay and study!

Ach! What university? What good is it to study under bombs and limitations? There are universities in Canada too, girl!

Don't be silly! Use this opportunity to live freely while you're young! We and your brothers will support you financially until the end of your studies there

But Mum! How can you support me financially? With what money? I don't want to become the third child for you to be worried about! Two are enough! No! Please! I won't leave you!

Think about it one more time... oh my child.

33

I had tried to figure this out before, but she made me see more clearly, and I could see it now: language. I think one is at home in one's mother tongue. A foreign language, even if learned properly, does not pass along the emotional depth of one's message.

I can imagine that it's hard to learn a new language, especially at your age, but that was your choice, wasn't it? Besides the language, do you feel homesick? The way I feel?

Well...maybe. I think my answer is more likely "no"... but honestly, do you blame me for leaving Iran?

No. I don't blame you. After all, you're closer to all those who left me alone and went to the West. At least you can see them whenever you want

Yes, you're right. It is easier to see them...if it's joyful at all. We don't really know each other anymore after all these years, but knowing that they are around is good. Home is where your loved ones are

For years I was most homesick in my own hometown. After such a depressing experience, I could not feel it anymore as an immigrant. I had been vaccinated against this sickness once and for all.

...did you hear me? I asked how you feel when you listen to Persian music. Doesn't it make you feel homesick?

Oh! Sorry!

Well, no... not really

Sometimes when I saw young couples enjoying each other's company in public, I remembered the situation in Tehran when we were in our early twenties, and the religious boundaries that the government imposed on us.

Tehran Autumn 1989

41

My parents were very liberal, compared to the traditional mentality of the Iranian majority who never allowed their children to have relations with the opposite sex before marriage. I had had a couple of casual encounters with boys up until then, all with my parents' knowledge. But my mother's reaction was due to the social circumstances of the time. Those years, the 80s, were considered to be the darkest time for social life in Iran. The revolutionary guards were all over arresting political suspects, women with bad hejabs* and boys and girls who were together in the streets to find out their relationship to each other.

*Islamic veil for women that covers the hair and body

What my mother was talking about had happened to me a few months earlier, while I was still studying.

45

Apparently he had made up his mind to choose me as his wife for whatever reason, but it wasn't the same for me.

What am I going to get by marrying him?

marry me! marry me! marry me! marry me! Marry me! marry me!

A legal boyfriend?

The brothers who left me alone?

an art teacher?

a moral counselor?

Go and find out about his background. Isn't your daughter's life important to you?

Of course it is! SHE knows him enough! Besides, I don't like spying on other people!

a protector?

Only to be able to move freely in this society as a young woman?

or

a husband?

In such an environment, due to the strict religious rules, our social life was confined to the four walls of our homes. This proved too limiting for us young passionate people, and led us to make big mistakes with consequences for our futures. Like my marriage.

Yes, I do!

Alright. Now answer me, my Sister: Do you want to marry this Brother?

Congratulations. Sign here please

We were about to ruin six years of our lives by answering the mullah's question at the notary office. We were much too different culturally, socially...

I tried to explain to her that even in the heart of Europe, where people have time and freedom to make their choices, they still make mistakes, sometimes big mistakes. I gave her a couple of examples I knew in Europe...

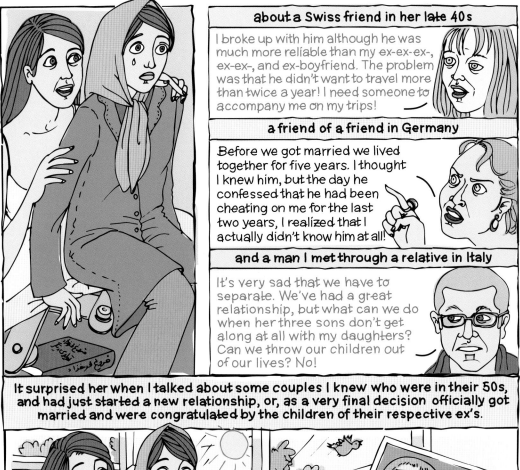

about a Swiss friend in her late 40s

I broke up with him although he was much more reliable than my ex-ex-ex-, ex-ex-, and ex-boyfriend. The problem was that he didn't want to travel more than twice a year! I need someone to accompany me on my trips!

a friend of a friend in Germany

Before we got married we lived together for five years. I thought I knew him, but the day he confessed that he had been cheating on me for the last two years, I realized that I actually didn't know him at all!

and a man I met through a relative in Italy

It's very sad that we have to separate. We've had a great relationship, but what can we do when her three sons don't get along at all with my daughters? Can we throw our children out of our lives? No!

It surprised her when I talked about some couples I knew who were in their 50s, and had just started a new relationship, or, as a very final decision officially got married and were congratulated by the children of their respective ex's.

Here in the West, people first live together to get to know each other better, then they maybe get married. There, in Iran of the 80s, we had to get married first before we could get to know each other.

I didn't know many Iranians in Zurich, except for a few from mixed marriages, or from the second generation who had never lived in Iran. But a Swiss friend introduced me to a young Iranian woman who was studying science.

Although there was a jazz performance, everybody was busy trying to be louder than the music, so we decided to go sit by the lake.

When she started I had to agree with her, although she obviously got carried away and hit a tone that sounded racist to me—she made me uncomfortable.

We **PERSIANS** were living in "PARDIS"—from where the word "paradise" comes— watching the game of "POLO" from the top of our palaces,...eating "PISTACHIOS" with "CAVIAR"...caressing our "PERSIAN CATS"...listening to the tales of "1001 NIGHTS" which the Arabs stole from us..."SAFFRON" and "SHIRAZ" wine...we "ARYANS"...the poetry...By the way! Did you know that BIJAN, the fashion designer in Paris is also **PERSIAN**?

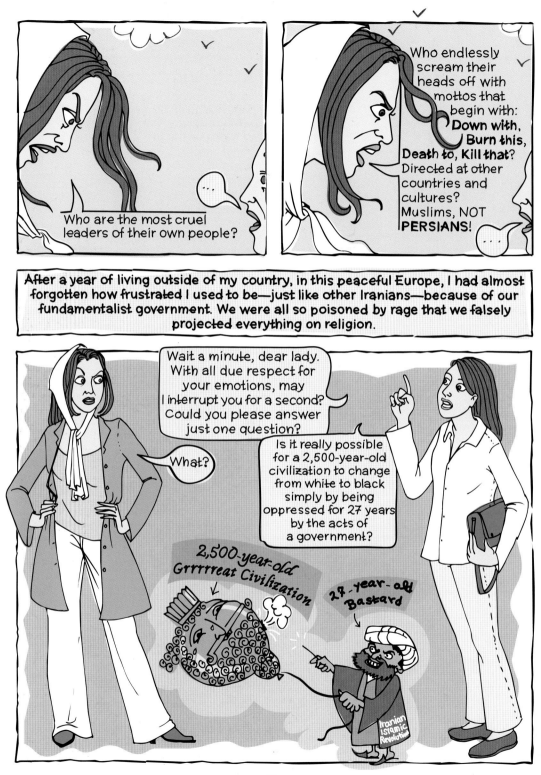

Who are the most cruel leaders of their own people?

Who endlessly scream their heads off with mottos that begin with: **Down with, Burn this, Death to, Kill that**? Directed at other countries and cultures? Muslims, NOT **PERSIANS**!

After a year of living outside of my country, in this peaceful Europe, I had almost forgotten how frustrated I used to be—just like other Iranians—because of our fundamentalist government. We were all so poisoned by rage that we falsely projected everything on religion.

Wait a minute, dear lady. With all due respect for your emotions, may I interrupt you for a second? Could you please answer just one question?

What?

Is it really possible for a 2,500-year-old civilization to change from white to black simply by being oppressed for 27 years by the acts of a government?

2,500-year-old Grrrrreat Civilization

27-year-old Bastard

Iranian Islamic Revolution

That great Persian paradise of hers might even have existed—how do I know?—but for 1,400 of those 2,500 years, Islam was the religion of these people. Islam merged with the Iranian culture and mentality to the extent that they now might be inseparable.

But people believed in a liberal moderate version of Islam before the revolution. It was never dictated to them from above by a hardline power.

Of course it was. What about Omavi, Abbasi, and Safavid? Just to name a few of the strictly religious dynasties...

I am not in favor of our fundamentalist government at all, but I must say that though there are enormous problems in Iran's situation today, we can't blame it all only on religion.

I tried to explain to her what I thought: that our government only pretends to be a religious regime, which I believe it actually isn't.

Have you asked yourself why our government insists so much on women's head scarves and banning alcohol?

What a question? It's obvious! Wearing a hejab and abstinence are among the most fundamental rules in Islamic law. They are the pillars of their belief. And this government is strictly Muslim; they believe in that!

60

To make sure that the world does not forget that they are the most holy regime on earth, mullahs make a fuss once in a while about the length or color of women's scarves. It's a trick, and sadly enough, even non-conservatives and the liberal press throw oil into this fake fire

Yes, the Iranians' problems are not alcohol or scarves. My people's problems are the oil-based economy and the lack of education, freedom, and democracy

Iran is on its historical path of progress, with or without an Islamic regime. Iran needs energetic and educated Iranians—and only Iranians—to speed up this process, much more than shallow patriots who give the rest of the world a distorted picture of our country

Once in a while I would see mothers who had no patience with their small children. It broke my heart to see children cry.

She was me, 29 years old in 1995; a divorced mother whose five-year-old was taken away in court because she had asked for the divorce. I didn't like seeing her. Not at all.

Due to macho-based fundamental religious law in Iran, which, ten years ago was far worse than today, men could deprive their wives of everything, even the custody of children if the wife was the one who initiated a divorce. She was forced to accept unfair conditions. Otherwise, she would be tied to her misery forever.

*alimony **dowry

It was useless to repeat over and over to the judge what I suffered in my marriage.

You were flirting with that salesman. I saw you

He was jealous, purely paranoid.

Your mother is a witch. She teaches you how to betray me. Forget her!

He forbid me to see my mother and other relatives...

Those women you call "friends" are simply a bunch of bitches. No way

...as well as all of my friends, women or men...

I bring home enough work for you. The world outside is full of wolves

f...k that

and I wasn't allowed to work outside of the home anymore

How can you let her watch this disgusting pornographic cartoon? No TV or videos from now on

Sleeping beauty?

It's only Sleeping Beauty! Man! Stop!

Mummy, what is por...I want to see my film...puh uhu

NO

And these were only details of the fundamental problems we had in our marriage. But these reasons were not good enough for the court. Besides, there was no way to prove them. I had no evidence. No witnesses.

I see you have not forgotten anything either. So how can you ask ME to forget?

I am not asking you to forget. I just want you to get over it. There are a lot of other people in this world with more or less the same problems, and yet they continue living their lives

I told her that even here, in the heart of Europe, women still suffer many unfair deals, though in a fair court

Where should we live? The kids are in the middle of school

I don't know. YOU are the mother. About the house, we'll wait for the court decision

It might take years for a court decision, and of course, whoever has the better (more expensive) lawyer, wins.

I tried to explain that even in Europe women don't really have equal rights. Although the laws are far better than those in the third world.

72

I admitted to her that for quite a long time I felt sorry for myself, which was just not right. My misery led me to fish for sympathy.

This time I was happy that I saw her. By reviewing our past one more time, I thought we were both able to forgive ourselves. I felt that the wound in my heart had healed...

But obviously not completely.

Among all of my new friends, there was one who was closer to me, both in terms of age and personality. I saw her quite often.

She is me at the age of 36
2002

She lived alone in Tehran and ran her own graphic design studio. She had to work hard to make a living, but was active, successful and independent.

Therefore, very proud ...

almost arrogant

I almost always enjoyed her company. We had grown-up conversations about life, society, our plans and concerns. We both enjoyed it.

We had a lot of fun exchanging opinions on advertising and magazine design when we saw good ideas.

But sometimes I really didn't like being seen with her. She was embarrassing. She was loud.

She spoke about the strong women she knew who faced all kinds of situations in Iran and who fought until death for a better world.
I respected those women as well but thought that she was barking up the wrong tree. But that was the way she thought.

When we looked in bookshop windows, she couldn't stop talking.

Iranian women don't wear burqa... this woman is an Arab...apart from that, the desert, the camel...this man is an Uzbek! On a Persian novel?!?

She was right. But she reminded me of my own mistakes when I used inappropriate elements designing book covers and my own ignorance of the West.

But... Salzburg is in Austria, not in Holland!

Shit

Oh really?

AMADEUS MOZART "A LIFE"

Through her I was reminded that after all, neither Westerners nor Easterners know much about each other's culture.

I learned that not knowing is not a sin.
Not knowing and yet being prejudiced is where the problem starts.

I discovered that most Europeans like cooking and entertaining at home, and there are actually some very good cooks amongst them, both men and women. I loved receiving invitations from them.

Good food tastes even better when it's served on an elegantly set table. Even more so when there are candles, wine glasses, etc. etc.

A nice and inviting table changes the plain act of eating...

into a pleasant and relaxing event.

In such an atmosphere, thoughts, ideas and advice are exchanged over dinner.

If the weather stays nice, I plan to bring my patients to the south. We could all use a break. At first I planned a beach trip, but...

Darling, could you pass me the salt?

I could never understand why clothing companies change their old classics. Even though they are still perfectly okay! I can't find anything anymore...

...first you chop the onions, then you gently sauté them in truffle oil with the kidneys and simply serve them over the salad. The truffle oil is the trick. My little secret. And don't forget:

This salad should only be served with white wine from Sicily

...well, I admit that at first I was disappointed by Khatami, but now I admire his wisdom and patience. Well, let's not talk about politics! By the way, where do you get this oil? Truf...what was it called?

84

Of course she couldn't possibly know who President Khatami was; she was me in 1987, 21 years old. At that time, someone else was president. It was the last year of the Iran-Iraq war and Tehran was being bombed heavily by Iraqi jets—almost everyday.

In a way she was right. She could only see the extreme differences of quality of life between Iran and Europe, which she called luxurious. She could not know that after the war, things got better.
But back then...

But even in these circumstances, when there was either a shortage or complete lack of everything, families tried to keep their spirits up and quality of life high, in any possible improvised way.

Hmmm, hmm

Everyone is going to recognize your old bedspread in my new coat!

It was difficult to find fabric.

This one is almost an antique. I found it in grandma's basement!

The electricity went out all the time.

And there wasn't enough fuel.

Every family tried to keep company with relatives and friends as often as they could, since in company it was easier to feel solidarity and be less afraid. In different ways, some like my middle-class family:

I bet your coat is Christian Dior! Where did you buy it?

Madame has forgotten that the Shah is gone

I didn't buy it.

You see, my wife is not only a good cook, but a great seamstress!

You won the bet! I copied it from a 1979 Dior catalogue

Middle-class style

Stop picking your nose!

Yeah, Mashallah, my child

Traditional Style

meow

or in a traditional way like the majority of people.

89

Once in a while we even set up exhibitions at home to show our friends and university colleagues what we had done. We could have used the faculty studios, but that would have meant following a whole set of rules—like censoring our pictures. On top of that, at the university we weren't allowed to speak freely with boys. Without scarves it was more fun talking to them.

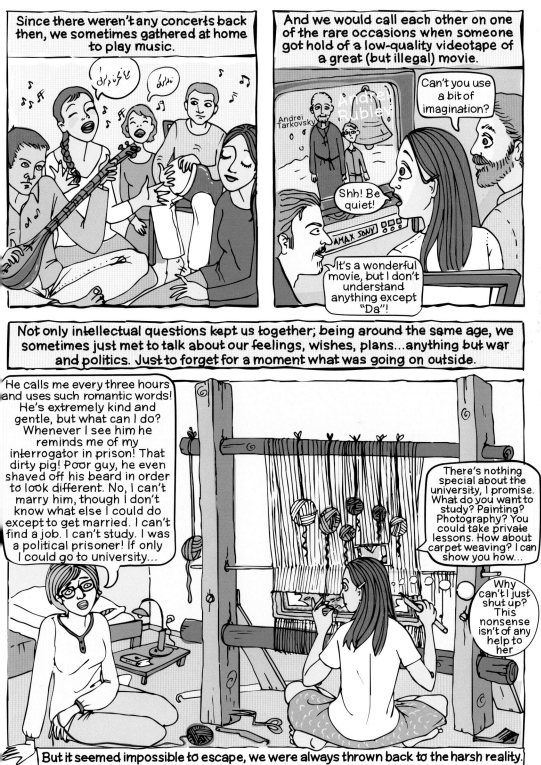

93

It wasn't always difficult with them. Sometimes they were the ones who helped me through situations with their arguments.

Oh shit. I'll never learn this language. It's far too difficult!

Schauen Sie das Bild an und lesen Sie den Text*

What do you mean "you can't"? With all these CDs and books and the computer you have? Have you already forgotten how my situation was in those days?

*Look at the picture and read the text

It was 1985. I was in my second year of graphic design studies at Tehran University.

FACULTY OF FINE ARTS LIBRARY

The art books had been censored with markers or scissors by the Cultural Revolutionary Committee. Some pages were even completely torn out by angry fingers. It was sad.

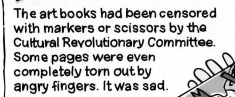

We weren't allowed to see any design or artistic masterpieces. It was like a vacuum: no visual or literary sources. But there were solutions to these problems, if you really wanted to see the un-censored books.

STORAGE

Oh really?

What do you want?

Keep Quiet

Brothers and Sisters must sit separately

Read the Holy Book. Cultivate yourself from within

Ass hole

Psst! Psst!

BROTHERS

SISTERS

I was telling my friends that you are a real gentleman. Everybody agrees ... blah blah blah ...

Well, I just want to go to the stacks for a bit of peace and quiet. You see what it's like here...

97

Well, well. Since this was only the first time, you are forbidden to use the library for one semester. Give me your library card. And Sister, your veil doesn't suit the sacred atmosphere of the university. It is too short

How could he see my veil if he was looking at the floor and the walls the whole time?

Brothers were not allowed to make eye contact with Sisters.

Even under those conditions where nothing was allowed to be seen or heard, people still found their own ways of ignoring the rules.

Home videos were forbidden.

Sometimes one of us could smuggle in a magazine from Turkey...

...or some "in" tapes from the black market.

I remembered when the graphic design students found out that if we wrote to American or European art and design magazines, they would send us their free catalogues and brochures with the price lists. Those catalogues were so precious to us, even though we could never buy anything.

Among all of those magazines, Graphis was always my favorite. So I brought her to Dufourstrasse here in Zurich to show her the Graphis office.

When the weather was nice, I'd bring a book and sit in a street café over a cup of coffee, but most of the time I just people-watched instead.

This time it was me at the age of 13, right after the revolution in the spring of 1979. The change brought forward various groups and political parties. These, along with the older parties that operated underground during the Shah's regime, began to absorb people quickly. Teenagers were totally involved in this exciting scene. Everybody chose a group. To me, as the daughter of an old leftist, choosing a radical communist party seemed reasonable.

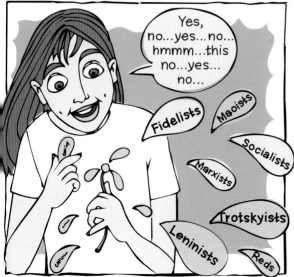

103

In order to be eligible as a member of one of the groups, we had to do a lot of preparatory training.

We rehearsed the leftist songs and marches...

...we sold the pamphlets of our group...

During breaks we held demonstrations in the school yard...

on rare occasions, we were honored with the privilege of working with the seniors...

*derogatory term for a nonbeliever

We had to read books, essays and pamphlets, as specified by our party's reading list. We also had to improve our general knowledge by reading tons of history, philosophy, sociology, classical literature, plays...to be honest, apart from the novels, I understood almost nothing of what I read.

But to help us understand what we read, we had to discuss in groups the issues in our reading. Since dialectics was the basis:

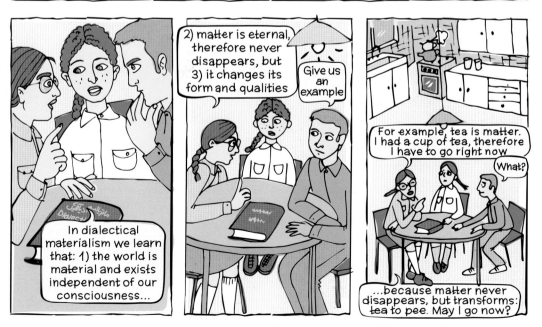

Then came the most exciting part many of us were looking forward to: strengthening our minds and bodies for the event of partisan combat or being captured by the enemy...

heavy

pain in the back

a balanced mind is only in a balance body

water bread

32...
33...
34...35...
36...

A very important part of the "self-building" process was what we called "self-criticizing" in groups.

...that day in the mountains, I hid behind a rock and had a sandwich, more than my lunch ration...ummm... with a cola

We also had to be prepared to be criticized by our comrades.

Bourgeois style

Shit

Comrade! I saw you yesterday with your parents. You tied your hair up like a bourgeois. You know how a communist is supposed to look, don't you?

Oh!

Proletariat style

We had been taught that discussion was the best way to convince non-followers. But if there was no sign of success, we had to take more drastic measures, namely to actually fight for our rights.

It must be said that these measures often worked well. I held a sit-in in the living room for three days, because I didn't want to share a room with one of my brothers anymore. The boys moved into a room together, so I won.

In June 1981, when young members of the opposition who had been arrested and held in prison were being executed, everybody went underground. For those of us who had already exposed ourselves, continuing our activities was no longer just a harmless game. It became a risk.

I tried hard to picture the similarities—cults and political groups are comparable. Both need fans: consumers. They must unify their followers, the easier when they are young. No individuality is allowed.

Sometimes with issues like "hip," "top," "cool," "hot," "sexy," or "in"...

...or under one of the oldest concepts of human history like "heaven" and "hell"...

...and sometimes in the name of "liberty," "equality," and "people's rights."

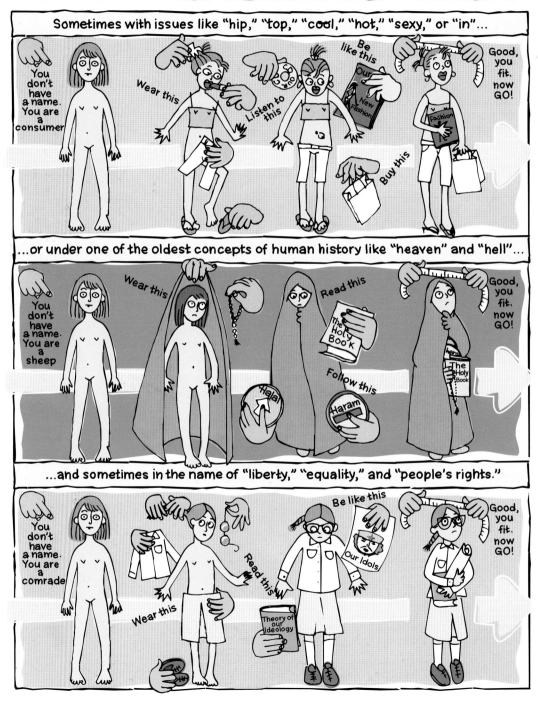

112

After moving to Europe, I began to look out for books about design, photography, fashion, and comic books. There were so many new things to discover.

In Iran, fashion magazines were strictly forbidden. Even during President Khatami's so-called Perestroika showing a naked or partially naked woman would have been impossible.

It was quite shocking to see such a title: "Colonial Girl." I couldn't believe my eyes.

In 1999, while constantly working on jobs in my graphic design studio, I was told about a fashion design competition for women designers. Being interested in fashion, I took part.

The competition concluded with a fashion show, for women only, of course. To my surprise, I was amongst the ten winners, so I had to start realizing the designs. I engaged a seamstress, and five of my pieces were even awarded prizes.

Ladies! Now the next...

Congratulations!

Thanks

AWARD
Sheherazade goes to Milan

This was my very first real experience with fashion design, making me alert and sensitive to the subject.

I tried to make original outfits by myself.

I was more aware of people's clothes in the street.

I was especially interested in regional and local Iranian clothing rich in design, color, creativity and practicality as a source for new designs for everyday urban life in Tehran.

With an eye on local clothing, I could add just one or two new details to a boring old coat and I had a beautifully designed original outfit.

The "manteau"—a long coat with long sleeves—and scarf are two main items that are most important for women in Iran. They became the focus of my designs. I was inspired by everything:

Mullahs | Men's wear in Kurdistan | Loristan Shepherds | Rich Persian paintings

ABA

KURDI

LURI

PERSIAN MINIATURE

This was why I enjoyed looking at magazines, shop windows and people's clothing in Europe so much. In Iran it wasn't possible to see anything other than manteaux and scarves in public.

But this was too much! "Colonial Girl"...HA!

She had a right to be angry. This is not fair to the Indians who suffered so much under colonial rule

Colonial Girl
Bombay Baby

A few days later, after I had already forgotten the colonial thing, she came back again...

Thank god she wasn't angry anymore. She seemed calm and relaxed.

That's why we Iranians should appreciate the freedom of speech more than anyone, since we've suffered from the lack of freedom for years...

especially women artists...Are you listening to me?

Yes, I am and I totally agree with you. And that's why I'm using that right to design my own fashion line: Sweet Slaves

"Sweet Slaves"

Cough
Cough
Cough

I've been thinking about titles like "Hanging Honey" and "Lynched Lady"...

Is "Sexy Slaves" better than "Sweet Slaves"?

...and as if it weren't tasteless enough already, she went on to show me other designs.

So when we're unsure it's probably better to keep quiet

especially when someone, like you, has no idea about the reason and background of a taboo, like the Holocaust for example

Do **you** know enough about the Holocaust?

Well, that's why I don't talk about it! Sometimes I censor myself too!

Oh please! So why bother writing a book? Why not just shut up? You've drawn us in your comic book, haven't you? By telling your story, you're expressing your opinion, right? You've said whatever you wanted to say in every other chapter. And you think you're censoring yourself?!? I have to say that your theories are **BULLSHIT!**

How can one be **free**

by not talking about certain things?

and what does that mean for the freedom of speech?

Award-winning project of Pro Helvetia, the Arts Council of Switzerland
within the framework of its swixx program.

For information, address St. Martin's Press,
175 Fifth Avenue, New York, N.Y. 10010.

www.stmartins.com

Editing/Translation: Teresa Go, Miriam Wiesel

Library of Congress Cataloging-in-Publication Data Available Upon Request

ISBN 978-0-312-53286-4

First published in Switzerland by Kein & Aber
First U.S. Edition: November 2009

10   9   8   7   6   5   4   3   2   1